Droplets of Spilled Ink

Jeena Chahal Dhankar

BLUEROSE PUBLISHERS
India | U.K.

Copyright © Jeena 'Chahal' Dhankar 2024

All rights reserved by author. No part of this publication may be reproduced, stored in a retrieval system or transmitted in any form or by any means, electronic, mechanical, photocopying, recording or otherwise, without the prior permission of the author. Although every precaution has been taken to verify the accuracy of the information contained herein, the publisher assumes no responsibility for any errors or omissions. No liability is assumed for damages that may result from the use of information contained within.

BlueRose Publishers takes no responsibility for any damages, losses, or liabilities that may arise from the use or misuse of the information, products, or services provided in this publication.

For permissions requests or inquiries regarding this publication, please contact:

BLUEROSE PUBLISHERS
www.BlueRoseONE.com
info@bluerosepublishers.com
+91 8882 898 898
+4407342408967

ISBN: 978-93-5668-568-0

Typesetting: Pooja Sharma

First Edition: January 2024

To my man
Aditya
My best friend, my greatest supporter who has walked every step of this journey with me.

Message to the Readers

Dear readers,

Within these pages, you'll find poetry that touches upon art, the human heart, the diverse tapestry of people, the concept of home, individuality, courage, self-love, strength, culture, acceptance, survival, and the journey of learning, all presented in no specific sequence. This collection is a poetic memoir, a heart laid bare, shattered and on the path to healing.

With love

Jeena

Acknowledgments

I extend my heartfelt gratitude to:

My mothers, Sushila and Neerupa, for their unwavering encouragement.

My grandparents, Shri Mohabat Singh and Chotto Devi, for their blessings that have been a guiding light.

My fathers, Sh. Rajesh Chahal and Shri OP Dhankhar, for their valuable guidance and well-wishes.

Aditya, Ashutosh, and Pulkit, for their boundless love and support.

Contents

HURTING 1
"Lost in Your Presence 2
Love's Eternal Symphony 3
Shadows of Ignorance 4
"Heartache Amidst the Crisis" 5
Entangled Melody 6
Divergent Expressions of Love 7
A Complaint To Rumi 8
Unwritten Chapters 10
From Darkness to Dawn 11
Echoes Lost in the Void 12
A Serendipitous Encounter 14
A Soul's Awakening 15
Fading Belief 16
Ink-Stained Solace 18
Guarded Hearts 19
Eternal Echoes 20

LEARNING 21
Resonating Strength 22
Beyond the Pages 23
Layers Unveiled! 24
A Symphony of Authenticity 25
Beyond Culinary Imperfections 26
Unleashed Radiance 28

A Path of Self-Worth 29
Liberating Heart 30
Disclosing the Enchantments 31
Blossoming Through Brokenness 32
Guardian of Her Heart 33
Letting Fears Dissolve 34
Liberation 35
Midnight's Spark 36
Celestial Testimony 37
A Self-Love Manifesto 38
Silent Departure 40
"Love's Perennial Verse" 41
Self-Sufficiency 43
Personal Authority 44
Unfading Melody 45
Amidst Cruelty's Grasp 46
Misaligned Expectations 47
A Dance of Uncertainty 48
Symphony of heart 49

HEALING 50
The Power of Time's Serenade 51
A Promise to Meet Again 52
Apology to self 54
Strength and Love 55
Radiance of Choices 56
Moon, Her Trusted Confidante 57

Forged by Society's Hand 58
Rediscovery Amidst Solitude..59
Healed Heart's Promise..60
Transformations 61
Serene Welcome and Farewell......................................62
Enchanted Haven 63
Destined to Bloom..64
Self-Love..65
Pursuit of Happiness 66

FALLING IN LOVE.. 68
Raindrops of Connection 69
Contrasting Worlds 70
The unspoken vow..72
Unforeseen Triumph 73
Vulnerable Desires 74
Everlasting Support...75
Love's Multifaceted Meaning..76
Celestial Affairs 77
Dreams and Reality Entwined 78
The Keeper of Hearts...79
A Battle..80
The Courage of the Fool 81
The Nightly Rendezvous..82
The Soul's Silent Offering...84
Immortal Legacy 85
Bound in Winter's Grasp 86

Captivating Presence	88
World Adorned in Beauty	89
Serendipitous Tale	90
Divergence	91
Her unbound self	92
Serenade of Selfless Love"	93
Silent Plea	94

HURTING

"Lost In Your Presence

I was a confident girl, standing tall and true,
Accepting life's challenges, I once easily knew.
But then, our paths crossed, and everything changed,
In your presence, my confidence began to wane.

Once, I felt deeply, even for the smallest of things,
Life's simple pleasures, the joy they would bring.
Yet, meeting you altered my perspective, it's true,
Feelings diminished, as if they were subdued.

Opinions once flourished, distinct and strong,
An independent voice, I'd carry along.
But your influence crept in, subtly and sly,
My thoughts became entangled, as if on standby.

Now, I stand here, a shadow of who I used to be,
Lost within the maze of your dominance over me.
Gone is the essence, the person I once knew,
In your presence, I've become someone new.

Love's Eternal Symphony

I have lived without you for ages, unhappy,
living without me, how could you be happy.
You ask me to leave you alone,
I think of leaving this world and be gone,
your shadow will flicker over again.
I illumine my home with hopeful lamps,
It is time for my darling to come,
I hurry, get ready to welcome her home.
Get up, get ready, deck up fast,
My heart beats faster, here she comes.
Her tears fell and dried on fallen leaves.
I bowed low and wept for her griefs.
Oh, the joke, those we gifted the wings of love
teach us today, how to love.
A home I built with blood and tears,
Her name plate on its door; it is hers.
Your kins scoff at my name,
Now, how do I impress them.

Shadows of Ignorance

He became a part of her life,
She fell in love with him.
He became unaware of her feelings,
But she continued to love him.
He broke her heart,
Yet she remained devoted.
He said it wasn't working out,
She was oblivious, it being her first love.

"Heartache Amidst the Crisis"

He abandoned her,
In the midst of turmoil,
Her mind urged her to let go,
Reason insisted the same,
Yet her aching heart clung on,
Unable to release its grip...

Entangled Melody

She ventured into love's realm,
But his heart belonged to another's helm.
Wholeheartedly, she accepted him as he stood,
Unaware he yearned for a love misunderstood,
Their story entangled in a triangular symphony.

Divergent Expressions of Love

They were deeply in love,
Their affection undeniably strong.
But a disparity in their love's hue,
When he arrived late, concern would brew.
When she returned tardy, doubts would ensue.

A Complaint to Rumi

Your verses paint love as serene,
But reality reveals a different scene,
Love can bring both joy and pain,
Complex emotions that intertwine.

In your poems, love seems gentle and kind,
Yet its true nature is hard to find,
Love's path can be tough and rough,
Leaving hearts wounded and tough.

Amidst the beauty, love can deceive,
Bringing both happiness and moments to grieve.
But within its complexity, love can be,
A profound journey, for all to see.

Unwritten Chapters

Together in one book we'll stay,
Yet pages of emptiness pave the way,
A gap remains, void and wide,
Created by your actions, I can't hide.

From Darkness to Dawn

He broke her heart, her world went dark,
Yet sunsets passed, igniting a spark.
She opened her door, welcoming the unknown,
And within, a beautiful change was sown.

Echoes Lost in the Void

Severed by distance, they stood apart.
He heard her countless times,
But failed to truly listen to her words.

Serendipitous Encounter

As a stranger he entered her world,
Unfamiliar, yet fate intertwined.
When he departed, leaving her stranded,
He became her entire universe defined.

A Soul's Awakening

His touch, a flame that set her soul alight,
Her heart stirred, destiny's tapestry so tight,
But now he longs to break the binding tie,
Yearning for solitude, love's fractured cry.

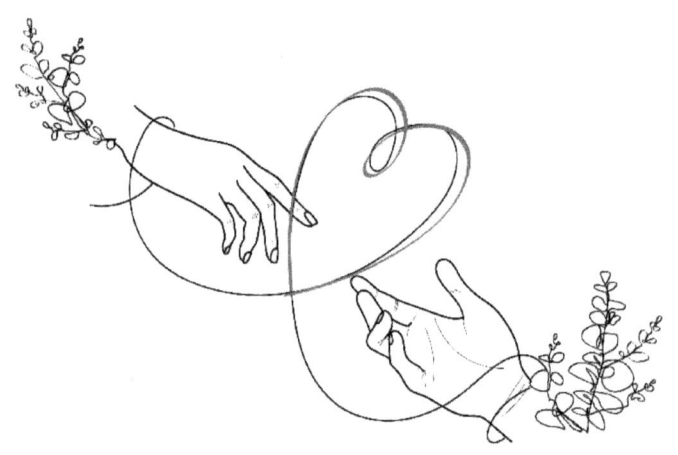

Fading Belief

Seeking faith in her own untapped might,
She yearned for someone to trust her light,
But seeds of doubt were all she found,
Snuffing out her dreams with no rebound.

Ink-Stained Solace

Ink spills, a sanctuary on the page,
Poetry weaves solace, emotions engage,
Through verses, her heart's secrets unveil,
A reset, where healing words never fail.

Guarded Hearts

Emotions hidden, secrets untold,
She remained steadfast, fearless and bold,
Undeterred, she pressed on, brave and strong,
But her tears flowed as he vanished, gone.

Eternal Echoes

Unhealed wounds, scars unseen,
Her pain persisted, a haunting routine,
She hid the ache, buried deep within,
Echoes of hurt, where shadows begin.
His touch rekindled the agony's flame,
Unleashing torment that had no name,
She carried the burden, silent and strong,
But the scars within, they still belong.
The wounds may linger, refusing to mend,
Yet strength resides where sorrows descend,
In time, she'll find solace's embrace,
A healing journey, with wounds to erase.

LEARNING

Resonating Strength

Within chaos' grasp, she found her way,
Knowing her voice held power to sway,
Amidst the storm, her purpose shone bright,
Her words uplifted, igniting inner light.

Beyond the Pages

She's an open book, inviting you to read,
Yet there's more to her story, beyond the agreed,
Unwritten chapters, secrets yet untold,
Beyond her book's cover, a tale yet to unfold.

Layers Unveiled!

I am more than
An Aloo Pyaaz ka Partha regularly eaten,
Beyond the pratha's taste, there is a broader view,
Lost stories and roads left unseen,
These buttery fingers, not all that I've been,
Scratch the surface and encounter what lies beneath,
A deeper connection, where my essence breathes.

Symphony of Authenticity

I won't be the ordinary girl in a crowd,
Gazed at casually in clubs or bars, disallowed.
Trust me, I won't judge him by material things,
His house or his car, no worth it brings.

I may be messy, order I don't maintain,
Housekeeping's not my forte, that's plain.
But that's who I am, and he must see,
To spend his life with me,
he'll accept my idiosyncrasy.

Beyond Culinary Imperfections

At times, I may falter in cooking or unintentionally scorch a dish,

But should these mishaps define me,

I wish to challenge this notion.

Within my humble heart,

Love, emotions, and honesty intermingle,

creating a different potion.

Unleashed Radiance

Beauty knows no boundaries,
In all sizes, it thrives,
Emotions dance within,
Where hidden strength resides.

Women, diverse and unique,
In their bloom, they inspire,
Their hearts hold intricate tales,
In hidden rooms, they acquire.

A Path of Self-Worth

In the depths of my heart, I decree,

Love's journey may challenge me,

But I'll cherish self and hug love's wealth,

For I deserve abundant love and heartfelt health.

Liberating Heart

Love transcends compromise,
its essence remains pure and true,
Those who argue otherwise,
mask the lies they spew.
For love demands no toll,
Sacrifice is a falsehood to be dismissed,
To label them as dishonest,
I will not hesitate to insist.
Those who speak of love's cost,
are misguided in their perception,
True love knows no bounds,
it flows without deception.
No price needs to be paid,
no souls need be misled,
Love is freely given and received,
unburdened, unrestricted.

Disclosing the Enchantments

In nature's realm, wonders unfold,
Miracles, unseen, in moments untold.
Near they may be, yet hidden from view,
Love, our guide, reveals what is true.
As we journey on, with hearts all aglow,
Unveiling mysteries, only love can bestow.

Blossoming Through Brokenness

In the depths of her broken heart, she found strength,
A reservoir of resilience that forever changed her,
Amidst the trials and tribulations, she discovered,
Valuable lessons and wisdom, woven within her grief.

Guardian of Her Heart

She radiates love, deserving of its purest form,
Her affection knows no limits, a boundless storm,
But only the one who treasures and reveres,
With deep respect and understanding sincere,
Earns the privilege to hold her heart so dear.

Letting Fears Dissolve

Yes, fear resides within, that's true,
Fear of judgment,
of losing my way too,
Fear of loneliness,
the crowd's overwhelming noise,
Fear of your anger,
of sleeping without poise.
Fear of mistakes,
of carelessness in my stride,
Fear of imperfections,
a flawless façade denied,
Fear of abandonment,
of rejection's cold sting,
Fear of suffocation,
where fearless breaths can't sing.
Yet, let me be, as I am meant to be,
Hugging life with ease, wild and free,
For in the absence of fear, my spirit can soar,
Unveiling the essence I've been longing for.

Liberation

She chose not to be oppressed,
Her freedom, no longer suppressed.
With resolute strength, she declared,
No one would control or ensnare.

In that moment, her spirit soared,
Liberation's essence, she adored.
Breaking free from societal chains,
Holding autonomy, no more restraints.

Her freedom began with that resolute choice,
To rise above, and not be oppressed anymore.
An anthem of liberation echoed through her soul,
As she claimed her worth and let her spirit soar.

Midnight's Spark

In the realm of darkness, she arrived,
As the midnight hour claimed the sky.
Yet within her being, hope arose,
A radiant light that refused to comply.

Amidst the shadows that surrounded,
Her spirit blossomed, brave and strong.
Hope infused her every step,
A beacon of light, forever lifelong.

Born at midnight, she defied the dark,
Her existence a testament, shining bright.
With hope as her guide and constant companion,
She illuminated the world with her inner light.

Celestial Testimony

Stars reveal harmony,
Magic and science entwined,
As are we,
Unified, aligned.

Self-Love Manifesto

Self-love sought,
no longer askew,
Love for me,
long overdue.

Silent Departure

"Why did you go?" he pleaded, voice low,
"Wasn't our love meant to forever grow?"
"Fear never hindered my love," she admitted,
"But it kept us confined, our connection limited."
Their words echoed with hearts torn apart,
A dialogue of shattered love, a painful start.
He sought understanding, bewildered and pained,
While she carried a wounded heart, love restrained.

"Love's Perennial Verse"

In the verses she penned,

Her love sought solace,

Aware that within poetry's realm,

It could transcend eternally.

Self-Sufficiency

Inward she turned,
Prioritising her own needs.
No longer striving to please,
She unleashed self-sufficiency's seeds.

Personal Authority

She whispered softly, a steadfast vow,
Deep within, determination avowed.
Taking the reins, her path to define,
Free from the expectations that confine.
With resolute strength, she stood with pride,
Breaking away from societal tide.
Claiming autonomy, her spirit unfurled,
To rule her life, with her own self in the world.

Unfading Melody

Love remains untarnished, let it be,
One betrayal doesn't stain its decree.
Inherently pure, it transcends the strife,
A faithful guide through the journey of life.

Amidst Cruelty's Grasp

In cruelty's clasp, your presence lingers,
Yet I'll face your malice with gentle fingers.
Heart and mind, harmonious in speech,
Within, we'll humbly seek the solution to reach.
You may be cruel, but strength will endure,
With serenity, I'll navigate and ensure,
Together, we'll confront this troubled space,
As heart whispers to brain, finding solace.

Misaligned Expectations

He envisioned her as a delicate rose,
While she sought the vibrance of a sunflower,
He clung to his perception, unwilling to let go,
But she, with a heavy heart, released their tether.

Their visions clashed, desires askew,
One longing for a rose, the other for a different hue,
Unable to reconcile their contrasting needs,
She chose to part ways, setting both hearts free.

Dance of Uncertainty

Betrayal's shadow haunted her heart,
His commitment remained elusive, apart.
He never approached, never drew near,
Yet she lingered, refusing to disappear.

With hopeful anticipation, she stayed,
Believing their paths would converge someday.
Love's serendipity, an encounter divine,
To make him stay, her fervent design.

In this delicate dance of intertwined fate,
She held onto hope, refusing to abate.
Yearning for the moment their love would ignite,
When their paths would align, shining bright.

Symphony of heart

Their love, a melody that sways,
Not there at the inception's dawn,
Nor destined to endure till the end of days,
Yet within the interlude, its presence drawn.

A dance that starts and fades away,
In the spaces between the notes they share,
A fragile cadence, a transient display,
Love's symphony whispers in the air.

It blooms in the in-between, their souls collide,
Where beginnings merge with endings near,
Moments cherished, where hearts reside,
Love's whispers echo, soft and clear.

HEALING

Power of Time's Serenade

Within Time's grasp, knowledge may reside,
Release control and let its currents guide,
With mending touch, it heals your soul,
In its embrace, growth takes its toll,
Trust the process,
And surrender to its role.

A Promise to Meet Again

Let us promise, you and I,
In whispered words, beneath the sky,
Though details elude our sight,
Our hearts will guide, with love's insight.

Through the seasons, we'll navigate,
Spring's blooming grace or rain's gentle fate,
In the realm where time resides,
Our souls will seek, where love abides.

Amidst the symphony of life's grand score,
Our connection strong, forevermore,
Across the paths that intertwine,
Our destinies converge, by design.

So let us pledge, with hearts aglow,
To meet again, when the stars bestow,
A moment destined to reunite,
Our souls entwined, in love's pure light.

Apology to self

Once, she chose to grant herself clemency,
As she pardons him in perpetual decree.
In the realm of forgiveness, she finds solace,
Releasing the weight of past mistakes,
 she embraces grace.
With compassion's touch, her heart finds peace.

Strength and Love

Through tempest's wrath,
she emerged strong,
Heartbreak's aftermath,
a battle long,
Against society's judgment,
she fought with zeal,
Surviving the storm,
 her spirit unyielding and real.
With a smile as her armor,
 she faced the tide,
Standing firm,
her worth she never denied,
Living life unapologetically,
she thrived,
And in love's hold,
her heart revived.
She conquered adversity,
found her own space,
Living fully,
with acceptance and grace,
Her strength, her light,
 an inspiration true,
For she not only survived,
but loved fully too.

Radiance of Choices

As a flower, she blooms with grace,
A celestial presence, a moon's embrace,
Within her, a fire fiercely burns,
For she dwells close to where the sun returns.

Yet amidst these traits, love's tender plea,
She opts to embody elegance, you see.
Choosing poise, she adorns love's art,
A testament of her refined heart.

Moon, Her Trusted Confidante

In every place she dwelled, it was true,
The moon, her faithful secret-keeper knew,
In solitude, they forged a friendship strong,
Conversing for hours, their bond prolonged.

Love, loneliness, and healing they'd explore,
Sharing common ground, their hearts would pour,
With whispered tales, they'd find solace rare,
The moon, her confidante, always there to care.

Forged by Society's Hand

Society's influence, people's sway,
Time's passage sculpted her along the way,
Independent, indifferent, and bold,
She discerned her desires, her path unfold.

With clarity, she claimed her destiny,
Placing herself first, a priority,
Driven by purpose, her goals in sight,
She charted her course, embracing her light.

Rediscovery Amidst Solitude

When he departed, her heart was bereft,
Anticipating solitude, feeling alone and left,
Yet within that quiet, introspective space,
She encountered herself, with newfound grace.

In the stillness, she heard her inner voice,
Unveiling strengths she once thought lost, her choice,
Loneliness became a pathway to her core,
Where she rediscovered herself, forevermore.

Healed Heart's Promise

Her heart, once wounded now made whole,
No longer bound to inflict heartache's toll,
With mended fragments and renewed might,
It brings forth healing, love's guiding light.

Transformations

With unwavering faith, she held tight,
Open to change, hugging the light,
In harmony with life's constant ebb and flow,
She allowed herself the freedom to grow.

Serene Welcome and Farewell

In serenity's embrace, she received him,
Welcoming his presence with tranquil vim.
But with the same calmness, she let him depart,
Releasing him elegantly from her heart.

Enchanted Haven

In this realm, I take no cover,
Merely adrift, a soul to discover,
Within my own enchanting domain,
Where harmony reigns, untamed by pain.

No shadows cast, no deceptions found,
In this utopia, truth does abound,
A sanctuary of solace and peace,
Where authenticity's virtues never cease.

Here, manipulation finds no home,
Only genuine spirits are free to roam,
A sanctuary built on trust's foundation,
A refuge from the world's illusion.

So, in my arms I take this ethereal retreat,
Lost in tranquility, pure and complete,
In my own happy place, I am truly free,
Where the essence of truth is all I see.

Destined to Bloom

With unwavering certainty, she knew,
Her destiny, like marigolds, would ensue,
In the midst of anything, she would rise,
Blooming brightly, defying the skies.

Self-Love

"I've moved on," she confidently expressed,
Curiosity arose, a question addressed,
"Whom do you date?" inquired the crowd,
"Myself," she replied, strong and proud.

Pursuit of Happiness

She chased no worldly wealth or fame,
Only her happiness, she aimed.
In that pursuit, her heart did find,
Inner peace, a smile defined.
Through winding paths, she boldly tread,
Leaving behind what others said.
Unfazed by doubts or judgment's glare,
Her inner joy became her prayer.
With every step, her spirit soared,
In pursuit of what her heart adored.
And as she followed her own bliss,
A radiant smile adorned her lips.
No wealth could match her contentment deep,
No accolades could make her soul leap.
For in choosing happiness as her guide,
She discovered the joy she couldn't hide.

FALLING IN LOVE

Raindrops of Connection

In separate cities, on a rainy night,
As drizzles descend, a familiar sight,
Raindrops fall, both there and here,
Uniting us, bridging the distance, clear.
Despite the miles that stretch apart,
The rain will bind our hearts,
In each droplet's touch, a shared caress,
No distance can quell our connectedness.

Contrasting Worlds

He dwells in a polished world refined,
While I, a girl with rawness intertwined,
In my world, books and words unfurl,
His indifference, a source of jitters in this swirl.
Yearning for him to perceive beyond societal norms,
To hold me, unmasked, in his loving forms,
To hold me close, comforting my tears,
Seeking solace in his arms, dispelling fears.

An Unspoken Vow

In your heart, I have found my home ,
A place where our love is free to roam,
No need for words to express our affection ,
In silence I find the purest connection .

No written trace can capture the bliss,
Of the unspoken vow, sealed with a kiss,
Let our hearts converse in whispered beats,
Creating a symphony where only love repeats.

Swear not to ink my name in poetic verse,
Preserving our love, in an unspoken universe,
In the sacred silence, our hearts shall speak,
A vow unspoken, a love that remains unique.

Unforeseen Triumph

Amidst the fading plans and strategic schemes,
He arrived unannounced, awakening her dreams,
Her failures transformed into a triumphant start,
As she willingly surrendered her guarded heart.

Happily, she lost herself in love's tender hold,
Trading her heart for a connection untold,
And after gaining his affection, a victory was won,
A journey of love that had only just begun.

Vulnerable Desires

Before you, I yearn to unmask my soul,
Escape this chaos, make my spirit whole,
In your presence, I long to be heard,
To feel your unwavering support, assured.

Stay by my side, be my comforting place,
Lend me your time, in this intimate space,
Be the energy that fuels my inner flame,
And promise me, forever, you'll remain.

Everlasting Support

Amidst his losses, she stood strong,
Through victories, she cheered along,
In moments where neither came to pass,
Her unwavering presence was steadfast.

Temporary were the victories and falls,
But she remained, his cheerleader through it all,
A constant pillar, an eternal guiding light,
With her by his side, his spirit took flight.

Love's Multifaceted Meaning

In love's realm, definitions diverge,
To him, a sentiment that time may purge,
To her, love resides in him, steadfast and true,
Enduring eternally, their love's vibrant hue.

Celestial Affairs

She fell for the moon, love's ethereal spark,
But every dawn, it shattered her heart,
He, enamoured by the sun's blazing light,
Never seeking solace in the starry night.

They both understood the undeniable truth,
Yet unable to resist, they fell for her, aloof,
Bound by celestial allure, destiny's decree,
Caught in a cosmic dance, a bittersweet decree.

Dreams and Reality Entwined

She personifies the realm of dreams,
While he exists in tangible reality's streams,

'Apart',
their essences remain unfulfilled,

Keeper of Hearts

Those with true hearts,
 they always stay,
Their love remains,
come what may.
Through ups and downs,
side by side,
Their bond endures,
strong and wide.
Through ups and downs,
they steadfastly hold,
Their chemistry unbreakable,
a story yet untold.
For in the depths of their devoted hearts,
Love's power sustains, never departs.
With unwavering loyalty, they stand tall,
The keepers of love's eternal call.

A Battle

"Are you in love?"
the question was asked,
"Yes!"
she exclaimed, her heart steadfast.
"How do you feel?"
they inquired, with curious eyes,
"In a war with society,"
she replied, unwise.
For love can be a battlefield, a fight,
Against societal norms, challenging the night.
In the face of judgment and opposition's sway,
She stood strong, love guiding her way.

Courage of the Fool

Allow me to be the fool, I implore,
To savor the depths of love's grandeur,
I yearn to feel your presence, intertwined,
To love you unabashedly, my heart defined.

With hope as our guide, we'll take the leap,
Through life's tapestry, our love will seep,
By playing the role of the happy fool,
I find joy and bliss, love's eternal fuel.

Nightly Rendezvous

As she slipped beneath the sheets so soft,
A promise whispered, floating aloft,
To meet him in dreams, where realms align,
A place where worries fade, an escape to find.

In this ethereal realm, no judgment prevails,
She pours out her heart, as the night unveils,
He listens with care, devoid of all blame,
Fulfilling desires, igniting love's flame.

Beneath the night's blanket, they convene,
A secret rendezvous, a surreal scene,
In dreams, they dance, a perfect duet,
Where love's unspoken words, they never forget.

Soul's Silent Offering

She delicately placed her soul on his path,
With a whispered hope it would lead him near,
In serendipitous moments, their worlds would align,
And love's enchantment would swiftly appear.

With quiet anticipation, she took the leap,
Trusting destiny to guide their destined meet,
A silent offering of her deepest desires,
To intertwine their hearts, igniting love's fires.

Immortal Legacy

In the realm where love knows no end,
Their love persists, unyielding, my friend.
Through her poetry, it shall thrive,
In his vivid paintings, it will forever survive.

With every stroke of brush, his heart reveals,
The depth of their love, emotions it seals.
Her words, like melodies, forever endure,
Keeping their love alive, pure and secure.

Their art becomes a testament, a lasting treasure,
A legacy of love, beyond mortal measure.
Through poetry and paintings, their souls unite,
Love's immortal flame, burning bright.

Bound in Winter's Grasp

Within the tranquil winter nights,
Beneath the canopy of stars so bright,
Deep within her heart's strong hold,
Their love resides, as a story untold.

Through radiant days and darkest nights,
Their connection lingers like shining lights,
No power can tear them apart,
Because they're bound by love's unyielding heart.

Captivating Presence

In his presence, she felt a stirring within,
A whirlwind of emotions, a complex spin,
Unclear if it brought goodness or strife,
Yet, for a moment, it coloured her life.
Whether fleeting or eternally bound,
The feeling emerged, profound,
In the grand tapestry of existence, it tethers,
For what matters is the presence that weathers.

World Adorned in Beauty

In his presence, beauty abounds,
A magical aura that surrounds,
Raindrops glisten with joyful delight,
Waves serenade in harmonious might.

Snowflakes dance with graceful art,
His heartbeat, a rhythm of the heart,
But most enchanting, in her gaze,
A reflection of love's vibrant blaze.

With him near, a splendid sight,
Every moment shines with pure light,
In his company, a world so fair,
Where beauty blooms, beyond compare.

Serendipitous Tale

She found him, unexpected and unplanned,
When love was not part of his mind's demand
A beauty that touched them all.
Their hearts intertwined,
In a serendipitous dance,
No grand design,
Just fate's happenstance.
Together they found,
A love so profound,
Unplanned and unforeseen,
Yet, a perfect match they had been.

Divergence

Transient Desires, Eternal Longings
He yearned for a fleeting stay,
A moment shared, then gone away,
But she dreamed of something more,
A lifetime together, forever to adore.

Her Unbound Self

Enveloped in her own essence,
With an effortless sway,
He became enamoured,
By her unadulterated, authentic display.

Serenade of Selfless Love"

Perplexed, he never comprehended,
How she poured her soul into their bond,
Selflessly, she gave without expectation,
A love so pure, profound, and beyond.

Silent Plea

In the realm of scarce words, I feel confined,
Yet, if I may, let my voice unwind.
grant me the space to share,
As my heart resurges,
filled with care.
Let me share my feelings,
Without holding my back,
As our souls connect, intertwined in fact,
Let's face the world together, for our love's sake,
stand by my side,
And lend your voice to our story
Let me express, let our love be known,
Together we'll face the world, hand in hand, grown.

Thank you

I want to express my deep gratitude for your commitment to obtaining, embracing, and thoroughly exploring the pages of this book. Your support is beyond measure, and it means the world to me.

As we approach the final chapters, I hope the ink that has found its way onto these pages serves as a wellspring of inspiration for your heart and a catalyst for your artistic expression. Your engagement with this text brings it to life and imbues significance into the words it contains. It underscores the profound connection between creator and reader, and I truly appreciate the role you've played in this journey. May the spilled ink ignite your creative spark and nourish your spirit.

(Poet's Note)

www.ingramcontent.com/pod-product-compliance
Lightning Source LLC
LaVergne TN
LVHW061555070526
838199LV00077B/7054